# Geothermal, Biomass, and Hydrogen

## by Jim Ollhoff

# Visit us at

## WWW.ABDOPUBLISHING.COM

Published by ABDO Publishing Company, 8000 West 78th Street, Suite 310, Edina, MN 55439. Copyright ©2010 by Abdo Consulting Group, Inc. International copyrights reserved in all countries. No part of this book may be reproduced in any form without written permission from the publisher. ABDO & Daughters™ is a trademark and logo of ABDO Publishing Company.

Printed in the United States of America, North Mankato, Minnesota.
112009
012010

 PRINTED ON RECYCLED PAPER

**Editor:** John Hamilton
**Graphic Design:** John Hamilton
**Cover Photos:** Jupiter Images, iStockphoto
**Interior Photo:** Corbis, p. 7; Getty Images, p. 11, 17, 19; iStockphoto, p. 1, 5, 6, 8, 9, 12, 13, 15, 16, 32; John Hamilton, p. 6; Photo Researchers, p.; 18, 21, 22, 23, 25, 27, 28, 29.

Library of Congress Cataloging-in-Publication Data

Ollhoff, Jim, 1959-
　Geothermal, biomass, and hydrogen / Jim Ollhoff.
　　p. cm. -- (Future energy)
　Includes index.
　ISBN 978-1-60453-937-0
　1. Renewable energy sources--Juvenile literature. I. Title.
　TJ808.2.O445 2010
　333.79'4--dc22
　　　　　　2009029864

# Contents

# Alternative Energy

The world is in crisis. We burn coal, oil, and natural gas in record amounts to meet an ever-increasing hunger for electricity. Burning fossil fuels damages the environment and changes our climate. Further, scientists know that fossil fuels will eventually run out. New ways to make electricity are needed, and they are needed now.

Solar power, wind power, and hydropower are three alternative ways to generate electricity. They are renewable sources of energy. The sun, wind, and water will never run out, and they produce very few environmental problems.

Geothermal, biomass, and hydrogen are also renewable energy sources. The technology to use them is relatively new, and not as well known. Geothermal energy has been around for a while, but it is underused. Biomass energy is currently being tried in a variety of ways. Hydrogen fuel is new and not fully researched.

These alternative energy sources are very promising, but much work needs to be done. Can the problems of a world in crisis be solved with geothermal, biomass, and hydrogen power?

*Facing page:*
A complex set of pipes and containers at a geothermal power plant. In many countries, such as Iceland, geothermal energy supplies a sizable percentage of their heating and electricity needs.

# Geothermal

About 33,000 feet (10,058 meters) underground, there is a layer of rock that is so hot it stays liquid all the time. This rock is called magma. Sometimes the magma gets closer to the earth's surface. The heat from the magma rises, heating the rocks above it. These hot rocks are found in seismically active areas with a lot of earthquakes and volcanoes. Water seeps down into these hot spots, and then turns to steam. Geysers like Old Faithful in Wyoming's Yellowstone National Park shoot up because groundwater has become superheated. Geothermal power plants can make use of this heat.

Geothermal power plants drill deep holes, and then inject water down into the pits. The hot rocks superheat the water, turning it to steam and making it rise to the surface. The steam is then collected and used to drive turbines, which power generators used to make electricity.

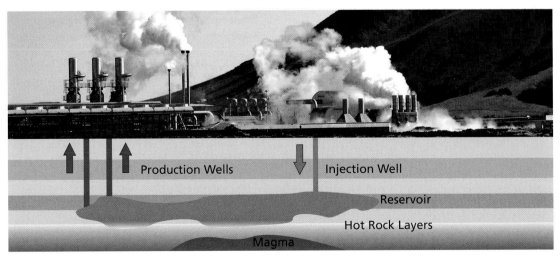

Production Wells

Injection Well

Reservoir

Hot Rock Layers

Magma

Early geothermal plants allowed the steam to escape into the air. However, sometimes it would become polluted with small amounts of arsenic or hydrogen sulfide, which are present in the hot rocks below the surface. Today, most geothermal plants recycle the steam. It is cooled and turned back into water, then routed back underground to repeat the process.

Only a small fraction of the earth's geothermal resources are being used to generate electricity. About 5 percent of California's power comes from geothermal energy. Much of the western United States has the potential for geothermal energy, but little has been developed. Mostly, this is because fossil fuels are relatively inexpensive here. Some other countries have well-developed geothermal industries. Iceland uses geothermal energy for more than half of its energy needs.

*Below:* An aerial view of a geothermal power plant in Iceland.

In North America today, geothermal heat is available in most of the western United States, western Canada, Alaska, and parts of Texas and Louisiana. There are a few states in the northeastern United States that have geothermal potential. Researchers are now experimenting with how to use geothermal energy in regions that are not seismic hot spots. Scientists in Japan, Europe, and Australia are trying to find ways to use the earth's heat any place on the planet.

More geothermal power plants will probably be built along the West Coast of North America. Some researchers believe that geothermal energy could easily provide 10 percent or more of North America's electricity needs. And if researchers are successful in developing ways to use the heat of the earth in non-seismic areas, geothermal power plants could spring up anywhere they are needed.

*Below:* Engineers discuss plans at a geothermal power plant. Geothermal energy could provide much of North America's need for electricity in the future.

# What is Biomass?

Biomass is any kind of plant or animal waste that can be burned for fuel. For most of history, the most common kind of biomass fuel was wood. People burned wood for heat, light, and cooking. In many underdeveloped parts of the world, wood is still the most common type of fuel.

Plant and animal waste can be made into different kinds of fuels. Biomass can be converted into a liquid, forming fuels such as ethanol and biodiesel. Many scientists have high hopes that algae will become a fuel source. Plant and animal waste—garbage—can also be burned as another kind of biomass energy source. Finally, methane, which is a gas that is released from rotting plants and animal waste matter, is another possible source of biomass energy.

*Facing page:* Dried hay and plant stalks lie covered at a biomass power plant in the village of Juehnde, Germany. In 2007, Juehnde became the first village in Germany to become energy self-sufficient by building its own biomass electrical plant, which uses wood chips, cow dung, and plant remains gathered from the community to create electricity and heat.

Biomass can come from plants that are specifically grown for the purpose of fuels, such as switchgrass, which is a very hardy tall grass. It is resistant to drought, needs few nutrients, and will grow in almost any soil. Many scientists have hopes that vegetation such as switchgrass could be grown for liquid fuels like ethanol. In fact, scientists are experimenting with adding switchgrass to coal in coal-fired power plants.

Some crops, like corn, require good soil, lots of water, and lots of fertilizer. Some people believe this makes corn less desirable than switchgrass for biofuels. Crops that take a lot of care and feeding might not be economical to use for fuels. Also, many people worry that if a lot of corn is used for biofuels, there won't be enough left for people to eat. Will it raise the price of corn so high that people, especially in poor countries, won't be able to afford it? Scientists and politicians continue to debate this issue.

*Below:* A field of corn in front of a biomass fuel facility. Some say corn is a good crop to use as biofuel, but many worry that it requires too much water and soil to grow, compared to alternatives like switchgrass.

Biomass can also come from the waste left over when another product is made. For example, when lumber companies use trees to make wooden boards, there is a lot of waste left over. Leaves, bark, and twigs are unused. Some of that is left in the forest to replenish the soil, but some of it could be used for biofuels. Farmers use animal manure to spread over their soil to replenish nutrients. But some of it could be collected for fuel as well.

*Below:* Wood pellets, a byproduct of the lumber industry, are usually made from compacted sawdust. They burn very well.

# Biomass: Ethanol

Plant and animal waste can be taken from barns and fields to a refinery. Here, the refinery bioconverts the plant and animal waste into a useable fuel. One of the most common fuels is ethanol. It can be added to gasoline to run cars. Most cars couldn't run on just ethanol, especially in cold weather. So, it is mixed with gasoline. The good thing about using ethanol is that cars don't burn as much fossil fuel.

Corn is the most common ingredient in ethanol. Ethanol can be made with other kinds of biomass, but it is difficult and more expensive. Another kind of fuel is called biodiesel. This is made from vegetable fats and grease, and it is added into diesel fuel.

Ethanol and biodiesel are cleaner than burning straight fossil fuels. However, they are not pollution-free. Ethanol releases carbon dioxide, which is a greenhouse gas. The debate continues: Will ethanol create more pollution and carbon dioxide, since it must also be grown, fertilized, and converted? Or will it replace enough fossil fuels to be good for the environment?

*Facing page:* An ethanol processing plant in South Dakota. In the United States, corn is currently the most common crop used to produce ethanol.

# Biomass: Algae

*Facing page:* A chemist holds a flask of biofuel extracted from the lab's green algae processing tubes. *Below:* Algae are a wide range of creatures that resemble plants, including kelp and seaweed, but many algae are also single-celled organisms.

One of the more creative ideas for fuel is the use of algae. Algae is the name for a broad group of organisms, from microscopic creatures to giant kelp and seaweed. Algae produce oil when exposed to sunlight. Scientists have been experimenting with growing algae in farms, and harvesting the oil to be used for biodiesel fuel. So far, the results have been promising.

Another advantage of algae oil is that algae consume carbon dioxide as food. Carbon dioxide is a major contributor to the greenhouse effect, which warms the earth. Could fossil fuel plants pump the carbon dioxide into algae farms—taking carbon dioxide out of the air and making oil at the same time? It's an exciting idea.

The biggest problem with algae is that the research is still in its early stages. The process seems to work in small amounts. Can huge algae farms be created? Can algae farms make enough biodiesel fuel to substitute for fossil fuels? That's still a big question.

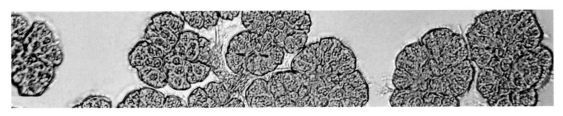

# Biomass: Burning Garbage

The average American throws away almost five pounds (2.3 kg) of garbage every day. What happens to all of it? People talk about "throwing it away." However, there is no "away." Most garbage goes into landfills. And these landfills are filling up quickly.

*Facing page:* Inside a garbage-burning power plant in Milan, Italy.

*Below:* A smokestack outside a garbage incinerator. Burning garbage can sometimes release toxins into the air.

One possible answer to this problem is to burn garbage for energy. The process works a lot like a coal plant. The garbage is burned, the heat boils water into steam, the steam makes turbines spin, and then generators change the motion of the turbines into electricity.

While getting energy from garbage is more expensive than fossil fuels, the process reduces the amount of material that goes into landfills. One disadvantage is that garbage is dirty. When it is burned, toxins are released into the air. Newer plants have strict guidelines about filters and anti-pollution devices, but there are still many concerns about mercury and other toxins that escape into the air. The ash left over after the garbage is burned can also be a toxic stew of pollution.

# Biomass: Landfill Gas

Any organic matter that decays gives off methane. Since garbage landfills are full of organic matter (paper, half-eaten donuts, pizza boxes), they eventually decay. Could the resulting methane be captured and burned for electricity?

The answer is yes, and it's already happening in hundreds of landfills across North America. The methane gas is collected from pipes and wells sunk into the garbage. Methane is like a fossil fuel, so burning it releases carbon dioxide. But without the landfill gas collector, the methane would have simply escaped into the air, so the result is the same. Some people say that landfill gas collection could meet 9 percent of the energy needs of some states.

However, there are problems with landfill gas collection. Landfill gas is only about 50 percent methane. Also, there are many contaminants in the gas, such as mercury, hydrogen sulfide, chloroform, and carbon tetrachloride. So far, these pollutants are not filtered out as the gas is burned.

*Facing page:*
Methane gas recovery equipment generates electricity at a garbage landfill in Boise, Idaho.

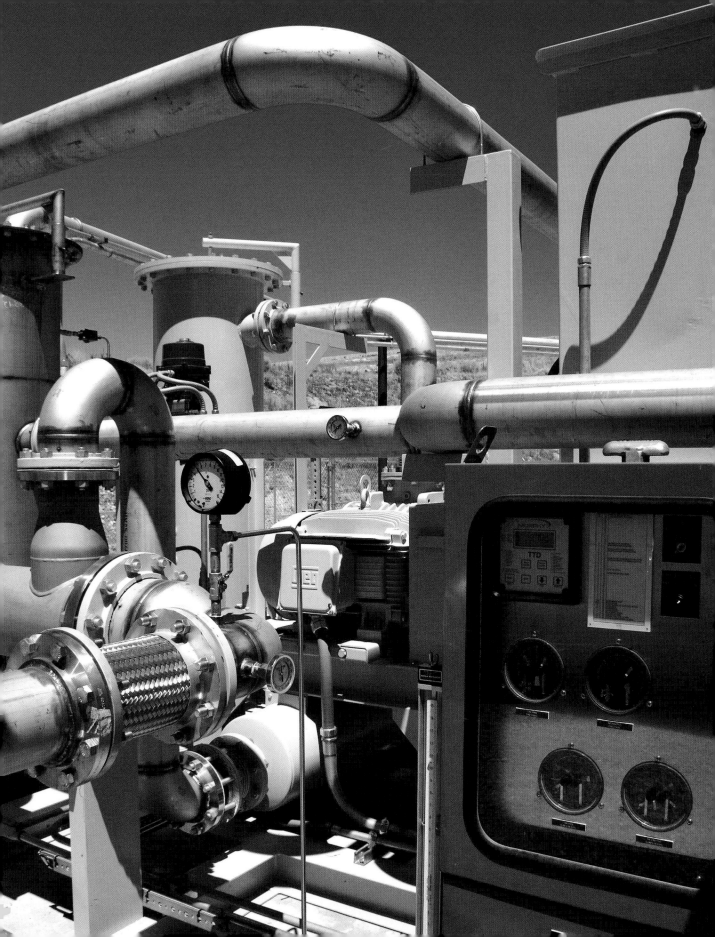

# Hydrogen Fuel Cells

*Facing page:* A hydrogen fuel cell. *Below:* Hydrogen (red arrows) is pumped into the fuel cell, where electrons are separated from the nuclei. The electrons flow in an electric current, and the nuclei combine with oxygen to form steam (blue arrows).

Hydrogen is the most common element in the universe. The sun and the other stars are huge masses of hydrogen, plus some other elements. Hydrogen is common on the earth too, but not by itself. On earth, hydrogen is usually combined with something else, like oxygen (to make water) or carbon.

Hydrogen fuel cells are like batteries that make electricity. Small fuel cells power experimental cars that are already on the road. Fuel cells operate cleanly and silently. They are powered with hydrogen and oxygen, and the only byproduct is pure water.

It might be possible to power a home or business with a fuel cell. Instead of getting electricity from a local power plant, there might be a way to get it from a fuel cell placed directly in a building. Every home and business would have its own mini-power plant the size of a refrigerator.

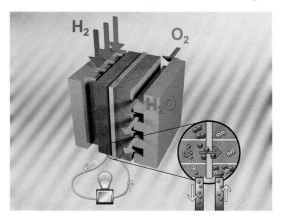

# Advantages of Hydrogen

The biggest advantage of hydrogen power is that it is carbon-free and pollution-free. The only byproduct of a hydrogen fuel cell is water.

It might be possible to use water to power the fuel cell. When an electric current is run through water, the water splits into hydrogen and oxygen. Simple water could create the hydrogen and oxygen to power the fuel cell.

One of the problems with hydrogen cars has been that there are less than 100 hydrogen fueling stations in the United States. Hydrogen cars are not in demand because there are not enough fueling stations. But no one wants to build a fueling station, because there are so few hydrogen cars. However, it might be possible to put a fueling station in every garage. Engineers are experimenting with an appliance that could make hydrogen and refuel the car overnight.

Many countries and many companies are working on fuel cell technology. Automotive companies are experimenting with fuel cell technology for their cars. Some scientists think that within 10 to 20 years, fuel cells will be available to run just about everything.

# Disadvantages of Hydrogen

*Facing page:*
A hydrogen
refuelling station.
The pump
dispenses fuel
for hydrogen-
powered buses. In
the United States
today, there are
not enough fueling
stations, which
lowers demand
for hydrogen-
powered cars. Also,
hydrogen fuel is
currently expensive,
compared to fuels
such as gasoline.

Hydrogen's biggest disadvantage as an energy source is simple: scientists don't know if it will work. The science is too new, and several technological hurdles need to be overcome. Right now, hydrogen is expensive to create. Scientists haven't found a good way to store it yet. Also, hydrogen has the unfortunate quality of exploding around flames or sparks. What would happen if a car or truck got into an accident and leaked hydrogen?

Hydrogen delivers electricity that is carbon-free and pollution-free. But right now, making the hydrogen fuel cells is a process that creates a lot of pollution. Can a better way of making fuel cells be found? How would hydrogen be transported? How would it be stored?

Can automobile manufacturers adjust their thinking to start making fuel cell cars? Can energy companies leave cheap fossil fuels for fuel cells? Can engineers and scientists figure out a way to make fuel cells cleanly and make them run cheaply?

Fuel cells hold a lot of hope for clean, renewable energy. But there are many technical issues that must first be worked out. Is a clean, cheap, hydrogen-powered energy system possible? It's too soon to tell.

# What Does the Future Hold?

Today, all of the possibilities of future power have disadvantages. Fossil fuels pollute, and supplies are dwindling. Nuclear energy leaves dangerous radioactive waste as a byproduct. Solar, wind, hydro, and geothermal power aren't being fully used yet.

Biomass is perhaps best seen as a bridge fuel—something that will help society as it transitions away from fossil fuels. Unfortunately, scientists and politicians don't know what to transition to. What will be the power of the far-off future? Fusion? Hydrogen? How about something really exotic, like antimatter? Who knows?

*Below right:* An atomic particle detector for the Large Hadron Collider project in Switzerland. The huge magnet is used to study antimatter produced by the collisions of subatomic particles. For now, using antimatter as a form of energy is something that only happens in science fiction.

28

If the technical problems with hydrogen fuel cells are solved, that might be the future of energy. There's still much research to be done, but it has the promise of cheap, clean energy that lasts forever.

The future of energy is dependent on the people who go into this field. The future of energy requires good scientists and politicians who can solve the many problems. There is a lot of work to do in this field, but everyone in the world is dependent on those who can solve the problems and bring working solutions to energy.

*Below:* A chemist creates cerium oxide nanotubes, which are only a few billionths of a meter in width. These new types of nanotubes may prove useful in making fuel cells.

# Glossary

### Algae
A name for a broad group of organisms, from microscopic creatures to giant kelp and seaweed.

### Biomass
Any kind of plant or animal waste that can be burned for fuel.

### Carbon Dioxide
Normally a gas, carbon dioxide is a chemical compound made up of one carbon atom and two oxygen atoms. Its chemical symbol is $CO_2$. Carbon dioxide in the earth's atmosphere acts as a greenhouse gas.

### Fossil Fuel
Fuels that are created by the remains of ancient plants and animals that were buried and then subjected to millions of years of heat, pressure, and bacteria. Oil and coal are the most common fossil fuels burned to create electricity. Natural gas is also a fossil fuel. Burning fossil fuels releases carbon dioxide into the atmosphere, contributing to global warming.

### Geothermal Energy
Using the heat from deep in the earth to boil water and create steam, which makes turbines spin to create electricity.

## GREENHOUSE EFFECT

The earth naturally warms because of the greenhouse effect. The surface of the earth absorbs some solar radiation, and reflects some. The reflected rays either pass back into space, or are absorbed and reflected back by gasses in the earth's atmosphere. Carbon dioxide is a major greenhouse gas that is produced by burning fossil fuels. When too much solar radiation is absorbed, the earth warms up, which alters climates around the world.

## GREENHOUSE GAS

Any gas that is good at absorbing and retaining the sun's heat. Carbon dioxide, which is released into the atmosphere by the burning of fossil fuels, is a greenhouse gas. Greenhouse gasses contribute to a gradual warming of the earth, which is called the greenhouse effect.

## HYDROGEN

The most common element in the universe, although here on earth it is usually combined with some other element.

## HYDROGEN FUEL CELL

A way of generating electricity, like a battery, that is powered by hydrogen and oxygen.

## RENEWABLE ENERGY

Any kind of energy where the source won't get used up. Solar power, waterpower, and wind power are examples of renewable energy.

# Index